Poet Tree

Collection I

Written and compiled
by Steve Petersen

Printed in USA

Copyright © 2017

All Rights Reserved. No part of this publication may be reproduced in any form or by any means, including scanning, photocopying, or otherwise without prior written permission of the copyright holder.

ISBN: 978-0-9960898-6-9

Printed in the US

LuckyCinda
www.stevenpetersen.com

Book Design: Laura Dobbins

www.stevenpetersen.com
Copy Rights reserved

PO BOX 932 Rancho Mirage
CA 92270
USA
Poetry/Short Stories

Welcome to the "The Poet Tree" Collection 1

Poetry, expressions, statements from people of all ages, backgrounds, and countries from all over the world sharing a portion of their "Journey of Life".

As you travel through the First Volume of poems and expressions from "Over / Under / Around & About "The Poet Tree", feel free to share your thoughts and inspiration on the open lined spaces in the book. If you feel like you want to share your expressions, please feel free to make a copy and send it to:

Steve Petersen Productions, 501c3
PO Box 932
Rancho Mirage, CA 92270
Or E-mail: **steve@thepoettree.com**

FORWARD

I recommend you sit with friends, classmates, groups or even strangers when reading this work. Feel free to pass around a copy of the "Poet Tree" collection with one another, sharing favorite poems, stories and songs.

I promise, it will be fun!

PoeTree
poeTree
Tree

By
Steve Petersen

The Poet Tree

... from the beginning

The poems you find here were written and or collected as part of the "Poet Tree" concept created in Palm Springs at the "Palapas Artist Garden" in April 1994. April is National Poetry Month and so it was perfect timing the day my dearest friends, Nick and Tree Williams drove me to Palapas of Araby Cove in Palm Springs to meet the owner Donovan Taylor. The moment we shook hands Donovan and I connected.
He said. "We're looking for a poet to round out our beautiful artist garden." As we walked through the garden Donovan told me how he and his wife Cindy had purchased the former Neel Nursery and turned it into an artist
center. There were artists from all over the world. Canada, Spain, Italy, Japan, France, Mexico, England, Scotland, America and many more.

We walked past a growing plot of Mondawmin or Indian Corn and cactus surrounded by a split rail wood fence. At the end of the path stood a dying Mexican Palo Verde. It had been a storage site for chemicals and fertilizers for the nursery. There were actually two trees growing about twelve feet apart with a steel bar connecting them at an equal height from the ground. The trunks of both trees had grown around the pipe until it was actually part of both trees. The Mexican Palo Verde is normally a pale green tree with fine deciduous leaves on long stems and beautiful yellow flowers that attract Humming birds and bees.

Both of these trees however were brown and full of sharp beige thorns.

There were no leaves, no flowers. Donovan looked at me and said, "What about this spot? You can set up here and we will have poetry readings and after we clean it up we can move chairs and benches for people to sit on. Set up a podium and lights!" I asked him if it would be okay if I cleaned it up myself and created a space as the spirit directed. I didn't know at the time that the Canyon of Araby was originally a Native American ceremonial site. After we stood there a few minutes soaking up the positive karma, we agreed that this would be, **"The Poet Tree."**

Over the next few weeks I removed the old bags of pellets, the piles of fertilizer and the remains of plastic pots and rotted wood vats that plants and trees had grown in during the 50 years the nursery had been in operation. I hydrated the ground, sawed and trimmed off the old branches. Next I scrubbed the trunks and put watering spikes in the ground to try and get the water deep into the root system. Within a month, the base of both trunks started to turn green and before long small yellow blossoms started to emerge among new beautiful green leaves.

The "Poet Tree" was alive and well. My next inspiration was how to display the poems I was writing as I sat under the tree. I found a bargain on five by seven and eight by ten solid oak picture frames. Depending on the size of the poem I would cut the paper to fit the frame and began to frame each poem. Once framed I glued the frames back to back so no matter what side of the double frame you saw there was a poem. I screwed steel eyes in the tops of the frames then ran natural twine down from the branches tying each end to a side of one of the frames. The framed poems hung like Christmas ornaments and blew in the wind like small sailed ships.

Wind chimes were added to the tree as was a hammock that hung from the steel bar stuck between the two tree trunks. Two of the Palapas artists, Steve and Kass Raich, crafted wood into furniture and artistic forms from ships to famous theatres. For me they created a wonderful sign on a great piece of driftwood with painted yellow/green wooden letters. It read, "Poet Tree" and was hung across the main "Y" in the largest of the two trees.

Soon other items were added to the trees; a bird cage with the door open and a poem inside sharing the thought, "If you truly love someone, let them go. The love they bring on each return will be greater than you ever dreamed".

Clear glass wine bottles began to appear in and around the tree with poems rolled up inside. The original "Note in a Bottle". Wine racks small and large were left under the tree and soon were filled with poems in corked bottles.

As time passed, one of the most inspirational items added to "The

Poet Tree" was the "Poet Tree Mailbox".

One of the artists painted the words "Poet Tree Mailbox" on a large white mailbox I'd found at a yard sale. I mounted the mailbox on a red wood post buried in the ground and posted an invitation inviting visitors to write their own poems.

Poets and would-be poets from all walks of life, of all ages, creeds, colors, and faiths started leaving notes and poems in the "Poet Tree Mailbox"

Some of the poets I had the great pleasure of meeting. Some I will never meet.

Many of their poems, notes, sonnets, and limericks are included in these pages along with some of the stories inspired by "The Poet Tree"

Take your time reading this book. Make notes in the margins, and on the lines provided. Write about what inspires you. Mark your favorites.

Send me your thoughts and poems.

If you wish, contribute them for the next collection. If you would like a "Poet Tree" in your front yard or town, please contact me and we'll see what we can do. At the time of this printing there have been 12 "Poet Tree's" built around Southern California. April is National Poetry Month.

***Thank you for being part of this inspired experience.
Love and best wishes always, your poet.***

Once "The Poet Tree" began to heal, the wonder of nature began to return. Humming birds and honey bees were filling the air and extracting sweet nectar from the flowers. Rabbits, lizards, road-runners, doves, owls, all sorts of birds and reptiles started searching for food and shade around "The Poet Tree".

Gifts and chairs, candles and pots were left under the tree in my absence. Signs of visitors became more apparent week to week. On more than one occasion I would find a family having a picnic in the shade of "The Poet Tree". One early Sunday morning before the garden opened I found a man sleeping in the hammock.

These observations inspired the poem I've selected to begin our poetic journey.

About this Collection
Steve Petersen

The writings you find in this book were created and collected as part of the "POET TREE" concept originally mastered in Palm Springs at the Palapas Artist Center starting in April 1994. The idea of an Artist Garden was to have a spiritual and creative venue where artistic energies could be expressed and shared with the public at local, national, and global events. Poetry, music, writing, dance, theater, and creative art needed a public stage. A more perfect place at the foot of the San Jacinto Mountains, upon sacred ground, could not be found. The setting evolved into a place where visitors felt moved to leave notes attached to the tree branches, leaves, and yellow flowers growing on the restored Mexican Palo Verde tree. The collections of poems, notes, songs and tales from the hearts of those visiting the "Poet Tree" became so numerous I asked one of the artists to paint a mailbox and I placed it under the tree. Poets and would-be poets from all walks of life, of all ages, creeds, colors, and faiths started leaving notes and poems in the "Poet Tree Mailbox". Some of the poets I had the great pleasure of meeting, some I will never meet on their Journey of Life. I have included inspired writings, poems, notes, sonnets, and limericks in these pages along with some of the stories created under "The Poet Tree." Scores of studies show poetry, music, dance, theater, creative and visual arts have become primary tools for teachers and counselors working to teach and aid in the healing of children, especially at risk youth. For this reason, I formed a non-profit organization to take the "Poet Tree" program to schools where children of all ages have been able to share their personal thoughts. In addition, educators have introduced students to the art of poetry through Steve Petersen Productions, Inc. 501c3

My hope is that you find joy, smiles, tears and laughter and that you will be inspired to create and become part of "POET TREE" Collection Two.

www.stevenpetersen.com
Copy 'Rights reserved
PO BOX 932
Rancho Mirage, CA 92270

USA
Poetry/Short stories

By Steve Petersen

STANDING IN THE DESERT ON the edge of an ancient garden being shown a tree of dying nature. Trunk and branches brown, burned by chemical abuse, neglect. From tip to root a dying Palo Verde, "This your tree. Make it live with words and work, poetic form, and we shall call it Poet Tree."

Trimmed, raked, pruned, resolved the toxin waste about the roots with haste. Opened up the ground, flushed water up and down from center out to all the limbs. Within a month, the green returned, with yellow flowers, bees sucked nectar from their heart. Doves, quail, a nightingale runners of the road soon stopped, to rest at Poet Tree.

A hammock hung with new framed poems and wind chimes announced by weathered log and letters signed by Cass. Bird cage with an open door, for love and beauty to be shared with all the world. Horned toads, lizards, spiders, ants, little plants of desert flowers and a young mother with her two small ones, playing on a blanket. In the shade of Poet Tree.

*"This is my favorite place in all the world. My babies too.
Like no other time, in a more than busy week, we come here
to share our love and dreams." A family Tree. Poems and
other gifts I have found about, and me a simple poet no more
worthy than a grain of sand, yet I share this space with
mountains and the gifted artists of Palapas, at Poet Tree.*

*Starting early to a Sunday rising sun I walked in reverence
toward the tree and in the hammock slept man wrapped
in burgundy. I stood in silence, hearing only wind chimes and
a beating heart. As wonderment consumed my thoughts,
he stirred. Looking directly at me, as he moved to sit he asked,
"Are you the Poet, of the Poet Tree?"*

*His gentle eyes and bearded face reflected peace and in this
place, a medicine bag hung around his neck across a dark
tattoo, a crest of his conviction. "You wrote these words
floating in the wind?" he asked. A whirl wind came from
nowhere moving everything in a flurry, then settled. "Yes,
I am the Poetry and the Poet Tree is me."*

*He remained sitting but spoke, "I am sorry if I have intruded
and will move on if you like. Currently this is my home and
I have never in my life found a more wonderful place to be."
I bid him welcome and invited him to stay. This is, in reality
a place for one and all to share. Who knows, in a world gone by
this may have been the tree of life And the man ...our Savior.*

The young man stayed for several weeks.
I found out later that he was a rising star, a concert pianist from the East Coast,
looking for answers before making the biggest commitment of his young life, marriage.

The Mailbox overflows

POEMS! POEMS! POEMS!
By Robert Wright (age 11)

Poems! Poems! Poems!
They can be about anything!
Poems! Poems! Poems!
They can be about
a chicken wing!
Poems! Poems! Poems!
Most of them have to rhyme!
Poems! Poems! Poems!
They take to much time!
Poems! Poems! Poems!
They're not worth the paper!
Poems! Poems! Poems!
Just turn them into
water vapor!
Poems! Poems! Poems!
I've had about enough!
Poems! Poems! Poems!
This poem thing is tough!

From the "Poet Tree" mailbox:

"Some dreams
We let go as we age
Other dreams
We hold on in hopes
That those dreams will come true.
Let love open our dreams for us."

Jess Clemens, Bismarck, North Dakota

Found on a piece of paper
clipped to the "Poet Tree"

"A saying from Zimbabwe,
(my favorite when life questions my
joy and faith). Love Pat

"If you can talk you can sing.
If you can walk you can dance ...."

Found in the birdcage, a scroll of handmade paper tied with a bow of weathered twine......

"Leaves form their circle......and seasons
find their Gateways...............Nor am I lost in you.
A breath of eternal wind to all ...." - unsigned

The following poem was found in the birdcage on a Sunday morning not long after the "Poet Tree" was created. The woman had written her phone number. I called her after I read:

"TRYING TO LIVE
TRYING NOT TO DIE
TRYING TO DO ALL I CAN
TRYING TO LET GO
LONELY, ALONE,
SCARED,
OPPORTUNITY LIVES IN CRISIS ...."

— **Leslee S.**

Ovarian cancer had been discovered in her body and her strong belief against modern medicine became a life or death challenge. Leslee survived and has been in remission for many years. She is strong, teaches and lives life to capacity.

"SCHOOL"

"School is rough,
It can be kind of tough,
Cute guys are rare
But if they get hurt, I still care.
My friends are a must
Without them I'd bust.
Homework gives me headaches,
 But I do it anyways….."

— **Kelly, age 11**

**Found in the "Poet Tree Mailbox"
wrapped in a yellow ribbon:**

*"I watch her as she sleeps. Her full lips and blond hair
falling across her face. I ask myself......,
'What will become of this beautiful child.......
Will she be like me? Will she always love me?'
With all my heart I pray, 'God show us the way
To always remember this day. The happiness we felt,
The love we shared, the memories we
made'........"*

By, Shelby Days Mama!

Please, take a moment and write your thoughts:

_____

_____

_____

_____

_____

*While performing "These Colors Don't Run" at a Veterans Day event,
I was introduced to a retired Canadian Major.
He asked me if I'd ever considered taking the poem "Flanders Field" and
making it a song. So I did some research and found out it was the national
poem of Canada. The Copyrights in the United States had expired.
I also found a poem, written by Moina Michael an American poet, called
"We Shall Keep The Faith." The poem inspired the giving of the
Red Poppy on Memorial Day in honor of those that had died in battle.
I combined both poems and created the song, "In Flanders Field."*

IN FLANDERS FIELDS

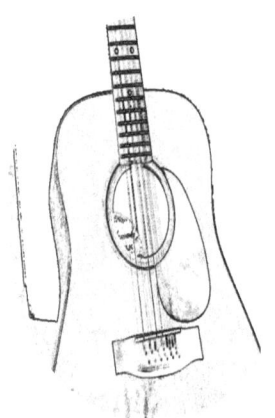

In Flanders fields the poppies blow
   Between the crosses, row on row
    That mark our place; and in the sky
    The larks, still bravely singing, fly
    Scarce heard amid the guns below.
   We are the Dead. Short days ago
We lived, felt dawn, saw sunset glow,
  Loved and were loved, and now we lie
In Flanders fields.

(CHORUS)
We cherish too, the poppy red
That grows on fields where valor led,
It seems to signal to the skies
That blood of heroes, never dies
Take up our quarrel with the foe:
To you from failing hands we throw

The torch; be yours to hold it high.
If ye break faith with us who die
We shall not sleep, though poppies grow
In Flanders fields.

From the "Poet Tree" mailbox:

"Sentimental Moonlight, fires that
light the soul.
Music to feel the passion……And
bodies
to burn like coals……….."

By Pauline Magee, Belfast, Northern Ireland

Found on a piece of paper clipped to the "Poet Tree"

"It's easy to see, I LOVE LIFE" ………….unsigned

Add your own thoughts to the mailbox:

_____

_____

_____

_____

_____

One day after a large event at "Palapas," I fell asleep in the hammock under the "Poet Tree."
When I woke up, I noticed the garden was empty. The visitors were gone and the gates were locked. I was now surrounded by nature: Flowers, trees, birds, bees and an unbelievable view of Mount San Jacinto.
As I stood in awe, a heavy wind roared through the mountains bringing a huge dark cloud right into the Valley toward me. Perhaps I should have been frightened, instead I was moved. I walked over to the stage and picked up my guitar and started strumming chords.
It didn't take long for the music and lyrics to evolve. May you be as inspired by my song, as I was in its creation.

A CLOUD CAME DOWN FROM THE MOUNTAIN
By Steve Petersen

Well a cloud came down from the mountain
And it came right up to me. A man inside
said, "Climb on in and we'll see what we can see."
We both got high then took off fast, headed for the coast.
I thought that I'd seen Jesus, but he said he was the
Holy Ghost.
From Malibu we headed North for the Polar Bears to see
But to my surprise they all had died from the poison mercury
We headed South o'er the great Rockies then on to the Midwest Plains. Where the crops turned brown from the solar hole and weeks of acid rain.

We sailed across the great North Lakes on to Washington D.C. where the Media Moguls command out thoughts, you spineless FCC. We saw New York where Miss Liberty lights the way to freedom's shore, to the Southern Border where a man-made line, swings free, cheap labors door.

Well a cloud came down from the mountain
And it came right up to me. A man inside
said, "Climb on in and we'll see what we can see."
We both got high then took off fast, headed for the coast.
I thought that I'd seen Jesus, but he said he was the Holy Ghost.
The last place that he took me to was high above our land
Where my ears could hear the rousing sounds of a thousand marching bands. The message here was loud and clear
We've tied our teacher's hands. Our children's futures are at risk, brave parents take a stand …

A cloud came down from the mountain and it came right up to me. A man inside said, "Climb on in and we'll see what we can see." We both got high then took off fast and headed for the coast. I thought that I'd seen Jesus, but he said he was the Holy Ghost.

Do you have a story?

_____

_____

_____

_____

_____

_____

NAME: DATE:

From the "Poet Tree" Mailbox...

"Love lives on in our smile n sparkling eyes.
Sky above, twinkling pond of stardust.

Cool breeze, hot earth,

Family peace
In an evening's deep sleep."

Carri Ann

ENOUGH
A pause
breeze stroking me
as the pen begins it's
story.

How could we
know?
Even now…
What's ahead
Just being together
is enough."

Signed;
MM
11-22-2001

"If I could be a flower for an hour
I would be a daisy, waving lazy.
        La Palapa is my paradise................"
unsigned

*"The clouds are laced with one's own fears,
Forever crying our lonesome tears......"*

Marianna Drake

MEMORY

I pulled back the shade to remember
    a kiss once shared beneath a shining moon
and glittering stars
A moment of passion so fleeting it seemed
nothing more than
a shooting star across the sky.
Leaving a trail of light back to
the wish of a man, granted from
the heart of a woman.
Disappearing as quickly as it had appeared
Creating a memory that will last ...
    Forever ... and the kiss was
ours!

By Steve Petersen

From the "Poet Tree" Mailbox...

Written on a piece of yellow paper:

"Back in Chicago, it's cold and damp
Here in Palm Springs it's cozy,
and I can mail this without a stamp....."

H E.

On a piece of Blue paper:

What a touch of paradise in this world of great expanse. one can take off his shoes and meander through the paths of life

Your energy is both comforting and relaxing, like
    this blue piece of paper.
Same as the color of blue expanse above us!"

Signed................SM

On a piece of handmade paper clipped to a piece of twine hanging in "The Poet Tree".....

I wish that love would empty into me
And everyone I meet............and
Everyone I've known..........
                    Unsigned.

...standing up between two rocks on a rolled piece of handmade paper ... under "The Poet Tree"

POEM

The girl in the Dream
My eyes shimmer in the light
My hair shines for the people.
I'm one of a kind, a girl I am.
People see the way I talk,
People hear the way I walk
I am the girl in your dream
You can release me now
I will be free.
Tonight's the night
I will come, so
Don't delay ... "
by Stephanie

....

CREATION
By Steve Petersen

When does a woman become a woman
At birth she is a child, a girl at fifteen
Young lady by her senior prom, the
gleam in a young man's eye, true
beauty yet unseen, until a
man with vision, plies
paint to canvas
words to song
hand to clay
and in that
moment
when
he
sighs
she
is.

Under "The Poet Tree"...

Hug a tree, sing to the sky, breath in joy, my spirit flies"...

Unsigned

"WOW
I love this place!
It's so cool."

Randy Mac
11 years old
"Great idea guys."
From Winnipeg
Manitoba, Canada
New Years Eve

... a note in "The Poet Tree Mailbox"

"Freedom is a word I rarely use without thinking………..Donovan"

Tied to a potted plant on yellow paper ...

"The sun is out
The birds are singing
The flowers are blooming
This is a wonderful place"

By Megan Klassen (Age 8)
(We are here for a holiday)

on a piece of folded red, white, and blue paper ...

"Overhead
There is a dark line
Beneath a blue sky
Always there
A line of ashes….
From the towers ..."

Unsigned

Share Your Thoughts:

On September 11, 2001, I was in Mexico
with my dad staying at our condo in Xtapa. All travel plans had been cancelled by
the international airlines. No one in our hotel could get home.
Two nights later, there was a knock on our door, we, somehow, were chosen for a
150-passenger list to be transferred to the airport for a flight to America. The flight
was operated by a volunteer crew from Pan American Airlines.
As we crossed the American border, flying from Mexico to LAX, everyone on board
started singing the "Star Spangled Banner."
LAX was empty. We were the only plane coming in to land and the
first plane since 9/11. I had started writing a poem while on board and when I got
home and watched the news, I wrote this poem which became a song.

"THESE COLORS DON'T RUN"
by
Steve Petersen

1). England came to test us long ago
The Colonists won against outrageous odds
The French and Spaniards too, saw red, white, and blue
Without a doubt they knew These Colors Don't Run

The stars and bars defended their own will
In battles where Americans were killed
But Lincoln had his say, in Gettysburg that day
The country came to know These Colors Don't Run

CHORUS: We'll tell you only once These Colors Don't Run
We're freedom defending butt-kicking son's o' guns
You threaten our freedom, a line of war is drawn
We'll tell you only once, These Colors Don't Run

2). Hitler thought he'd conquer the whole world
Put fear in every woman, boy, and girl
But American soldiers flew, the red, white, and blue
Then Adolf knew it too, These Colors Don't Run
The rising sun tried Pearl on just for size
The USA would not be taken prize
On the nose of Enola Gay, red, white, and blue displayed
The world had come to know, These Colors Don't Run!

CHORUS: We'll tell you only once These Colors Don't Run
                             We're freedom defending butt-kicking son's o' guns
                             You threaten our freedom, a line of war is drawn
                             We'll tell you only once, These Colors Don't Run

3). The White House told us lies about Vietnam
Our soldiers died but thank God not in vein
After a Congressional screw, we saw red, white, and blue
Our principles held true, These Colors Don't Run

4). Nine-eleven took everyone by surprise
The Al Qaeda cowards have run from our GI's
Over every hole and cave, red, white, and blue shall wave
The evil doers know These Colors Don't Run

CHORUS: We'll tell you only once These Colors Don't Run
                             We're freedom defending butt-kicking son's o' guns
                             You threaten our freedom, a line of war is drawn
                             We'll tell you only once, These Colors Don't Run

(New Revision)
Osama bin Laden found out, "These Colors Don't Run!"
NOW! ISIS is gonna find out…………
"THESE COLORS DON'T RUN!"

Next to friends, family has always been most important to me. Being a father is like no other experience in life. One evening watching the sun setting over the desert sky I reflected on all of the unforgettable moments of being a father.

MY CHILDREN ARE SOME OF THE ANGELS
By
Steve Petersen

New born smile, a parents pride.
    Mother's milk and sleepy eyes.
Tiny hands, a new tooth grin.
    First few steps, a bruised up chin.

Blanket cities, hide and seek.
    Candyland and muddy feet.
Leapfrog jumps, a lipstick smudge.
Fridge hung art, and chocolate fudge.

Backyard plays, homeless cats.
    Polished nails and grandma's hats.
Skipping rocks, paper planes, Little League
    Electric trains.

Soccer games, borrowed tools.
    Make-up kits, and broken rules.
A first kiss, the senior prom. A college town
    And then they're gone ...

My life has changed since they have grown.
    Once under foot, now on their own
        The memories surround my soul ...
My children are some of the angels,
that keep me moving toward heaven ..

Anything you'd like to share about being a parent:

Notes found on scraps of paper, backs of receipts, business cards, pieces of cardboard, under "The Poet Tree"

Aren't we lucky to live in California? Anywhere – seashore – desert – mountains – valleys It really is wonderful! Let's keep it that way!!" So much love." **TE, Laguna Beach Sue Higman**

"Thank you for having us. Love **Shelby, Lisa, and Chasen** We love the poet tree!"

"What a spectacular surprise is the secret garden

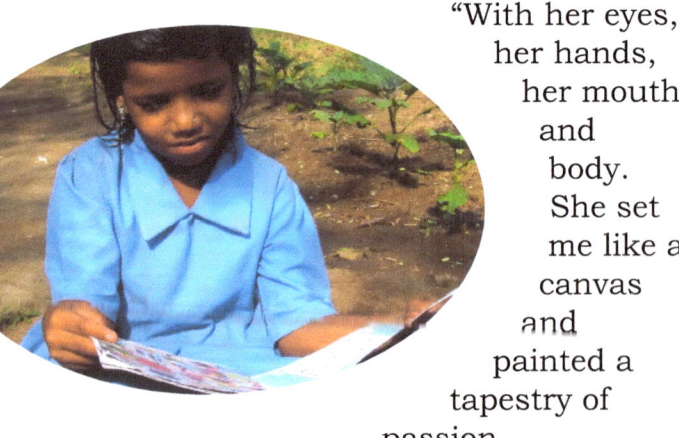

... and I say I'm not excited
  With my life anymore ...
So I blame the town, this
    job, my friends….
  The truth is, It's myself
    (mmmmmm) Dec.
      Heather Pitts
  (She wrote this on
    the backside or
    someone else's
    poem, crossed out
  her own writing and
         wrote,
'I'm sorry I didn't see the writing ... I'm sooooo sorry!

... **under "The Poet Tree" on an ATM Transaction slip.**

"With her eyes,
 her hands,
 her mouth
   and
  body.
  She set
  me like a
   canvas
   and
  painted a
 tapestry of
  passion ...

                    ... **unsigned**

BIRTHDAY WISH

By Steve Petersen

      h
     ap
    pyb
    irth
    da
    y

happy
birth
dayha
ppybi
rthda
yhapp
ybirth
HappyBirthdayBuy the candelsHappyBirthdayHappy
HappyBirthdayHaFind the cakeHappyBirthdayHappy
HappyBirthdayHappLight them allHappyBirthdayHap
HappyBirthdayHapA wish to makeHappyBirthdayHap
HappyBirthdayHaThe light goes outHappyBirthdayHa
HappyBithdayHaThe smoke is clearHappyBirthdayHap
HappyBirthdayHOne wish to keepHappyBirthdayHapp
HappyBirthdayHapUntil next yearHappyBirthdayHap

(Find the hidden words)

unsigned, under a rock, under "The Poet Tree" on the back of a Palapas business card ...
"Shattered Dreams, I thought I would…..ohhh……
Come on by. Oh shush, don't cry
Be strong and sing……….a song!
I'm so happy at Palapas, under the Poet Tree…..
You lift my spirit.
Thanks a lot………….."

The following poem is one of my many off-site projects. One being to place poems in empty wine bottles with a cork.
Some I placed in different spots around the artist center. Others I tossed into the Pacific Ocean from the pier in Belmont Shore. I tossed this poem into the ocean ...

SEA-MAIL
By Steve Petersen

You found my note
adrift ,,. in a sea of humanity.
snagged, heaved through straights and narrows rocks and furrows.
Overland, down sidewalks paved in stars of brass and stone ebbing flow toward destiny.

Addressed to you, without a name pull of Pluto, nudged by Neptune helmsman both,
from there 'til now.
Note in hand from handy vessel taken from the tide of man's creation.
What to do , my life so firmly in your hand.
Return the note to bottle?
Cast it once again adrift

You of such compassion,
Champion of Samaritans
take me in to bathe and sup hot soup ... !

(Follow-up to poem in the bottle)

One day a man called the phone number I'd placed on the "Sea-Mail" poem. He said, "My sister found your poem on a beach, she's afraid to contact you."
I gave him the location of Palapas. Many months later while sharing poems at an event. I found "Sea-Mail" still in the bottle in a rounded steel wine rack hanging in "The Poet Tree."

- the note found and returned

Hand written in pencil on old style paper rolled and tied to a birdcage ...

"Everyone is their own unique wave, yet
        We are all one sea ... "

Edward Torres

Folded under a rock ...
on a hand drawn heart ...
"Chimes
heat
wind
curiosity
setting sun
rising love ..." **Melissa Moore**
Thank you ... M.

BUTTERFLY
By Isabella Castrodale
Age 10
Just like a butterfly
My heart soars.
I discover higher
heights than ever
Resting on a rose during my journey,
And then flying away and away ...

Share your favorite memory ...

_____

_____

_____

_____

_____

_____

_____

_____

_____

_____

in "The Poet Tree Mailbox"

"With my eyes wide open-------
Today I shared a very special day with new and old friends------
Without this one of a kind place ...this dream------
could not have happened, Thank you!"...unsigned

... folded into a square and stuffed into a little box

"Dear Buffy,
I miss you. I will take care of you with God.
I love you, **Connor**" (Connor had lost his favorite pet)

Feel inspired? Write your thoughts

_____

_____

_____

_____

_____

**In 2006 the first "Poet Tree" was created
on an Elementary School Campus in the Coachella Valley.
This was just the beginning ...**

"The Cielo Vista Poet Tree"
By Steve Petersen

You inspire even the birds,
Flying beyond the sky,
We see from day to night.
Within your heart so clear and bright.
A love for all that see,
What will become of the Poet Tree ... ?

Since the beginning of the creation of "Poet Trees" on elementary school campuses we have completed 15 projects.

Once a "Poet Tree" is created on an elementary school campus, children are encouraged to learn the art of creating words into poems. It includes advancing their ability to read, write, share their poem as a song, and express their inner feelings.

Each year during April, **National Poetry Month**, scholarship awards are given to the top poets. To date over 120 scholarships have been awarded through a **Way To Save Wells Fargo Bank** account to teach and encourage the winners to save money for college.

Enjoy the following poems and expressions that were created by children as young as six years old involved in the Elementary School "POET TREE" project

THE MAGIC BOX
By Kelly Garcia, 5th grade

I would put in the box fresh
pizza and soda
from the refrigerator.
I will put in my box
the nice summer
day with plenty
of rain and flowers.
I will put in the box
the color of spring
and the light of the sun.
I will put in the box
the smell of my shampoo
and roses.

The box is made out
of materials and ice.
I will put in the box
the dentist's chair too.
That is what I will
put in my box.

BLUE
By Andrew Solano (age 10)

Blue is the color of the gleaming peaceful oceans.
It's the color of the clear skies,
Also, the color of the blueberries off the bush.
What have we done to cause these tragedies:
The blue mood the sad animals feel,
The blue butterflies falling to the ground,
The crying blue whales in the polluted oceans,
The blue jays taking their last breath,
The blue roses before they die.
Animals' tears asking,
Why did you cause this to happen?
Everything won't be so sad, If we fix this ...
By using cars less,
Stop making oceans filthy,
Reusing, Reducing, Recycling.
If we stop cutting the oxygen by cutting down trees,
If we help the planet,
The animals and plants will thank us,
For taking the sadness away ...
We can make a change.

GO GREEN
By Kenya (age 10)

Come on let's save the earth let's go green,
Think of all the torture you have seen,
On the air, on earth, and in the sea.
This isn't hard for you and me!

Not only are we suffering ... the animals too,
But there are some things we can do.
Stop using cars that pollute the air,
Instead use electrical cars or even bikes.
Animals don't have any other choice
They depend on us.
We need to think of them too, So let's go do what we can do!

Even businesses pollute the air. Factories, it seems
Don't really care. They say, "Go Green," but do they mean it,
Or do they mean, "Go Green" by the money they make!

Come on let's save the earth, let's go green,
Think of all the torture you have seen,
On the air, on earth, and in the sea.
This isn't hard for you and me!

MY EVERYTHING
By Jean Castro (age 11)

Father's hugs are the warmest touch, for that I love him very much.
He takes care of me when my mother's away, he's always ready when I ask him to play.
He works very hard for our loving family, to give us what we need to keep us happy.

When he is around we all feel safer,
he protects my family like a brave soldier.
I always thank God in my bedtime prayer, for giving me the most wonderful father.

Mother dear is as sweet as honey, her tender
heart is as sweet as jelly.
She may be busy at work all day, but she
makes sure I am always okay.

Day and night she watches over me, she
is always there when I need her company. Her cooking skills are better than the
rest, the meals she makes are always the best. No one in the world can ever replace
her, for she is a mother who is like no other.

My sister's an angel with a smile like spring, what beauty and color to my life she
brings. Her adorable smile puts a smile on my face,
she makes my sadness disappear without a trace. I play with her when my homework is done, when weekends come we double the fun. For she is a precious gift
from above, I will take care of her with all my love ...

LEGOS
By Sergio Camacho (age 10)

Brick by brick
color by color
hard as plastic
buildings can grow
as your imagination
reaches for the sky
helicopter, building, boat
no matter what it becomes
legos to megablocks
they both will always be mine

I WISH
By Jose Curiel

Oh I wish I could sleep or maybe weep
Or maybe rest but please no test!
I work on math, my science,
And I read every day
But I really wish I could go outside to play
I'm thinking of a way to get out of this
Please no test Ms. Jones I wish, wish, wish

REGRETS
By Emily Orozco (age 9)

Sometimes I regret the things I do. I want to go back in time,
And stop myself from making mistakes.

I wish to be perfect sometimes
Then I realize ... no one is.

Now I know you learn from your mistakes.
But I always wonder ... what would have happened
if I had ever changed?

FRIENDS AND FAMILY ARE THE BEST!
By Tatum Mahoney (age 9)

My friends and family Are the best,
They are better
Than all the rest!
My friends and family
Love me when I am good
Or even bad,
They cheer me up
When I am sad
My friends and family,
Make me giggle
And wiggle
Sing and dance
Get to know them
If you have a chance
My friends and family are the best
If you wonder why,
There are many reasons,
But to tell you will take me four seasons!
Help your son/daughter write what's in their heart!

Over the years countless poems were found in and around "The Poet Tree".
Many of them were not titled, dated,
or signed.

"THE MAN"
"Imprinted in my mind
Is a picture of the man
Pounding hammer to the nail
With muscled arm so strong and tan

He worked from sun to sun
Labored hard day in day out
He persevered through thick and thin
Though weary I've no doubt.

My admiration for the man
Is justly given for his deeds
He loved his family with all his heart
And provided for their needs.

To his children he told stories
Of his youth and of his past
His mellow voice raised in song
Made an impression that will always last.
The man has been an example
Of how a father ought to be
And I am forever blessed
The man is a father to me……..." (unsigned)

Found in "The Poet Tree Mailbox"

"I wish that there was more peace in this world!
All it takes is a little more understanding"

Jessica

There were hundreds of "Roses are Red" poems found around the artist center, this one by far being the most popular ...

"Roses are red, violets are blue,
Sugar is sweet and so are you"
From Vicky Maravilla

Your Turn, write your own poem:
Roses are red, violets are blue:

_____

_____

_____

_____

_____

_____

_____

... found under "The Poet Tree" on paper titled "Peace"

"Dear Fernando,
I hope you are not mean to me. You're the best brother in
The whole world. I hope you never leave me.

Love, Kendall"

stuck to a cactus
1/21 9:30pm

"I came so far for this,
Unexpected, only hoping
That my wish could be answered
And I could enter your GARDEN!"
Elina

on the back of a business card
"This place is magical" ... **unsigned**

And ...
"A natural feel is being in nature" ... **Santana**

Found in "The Poet Tree Mailbox"

"**PROMISE**
I can't promise you money
Nor can I promise you the world....
But I can Promise you I will show you how to live each day
as it comes and show you how to love yourself.....
    I know this may seem like an unknown
    dream or
    Reality but if you can allow yourself to
    take....
    A chance on you, I promise you, you
    won't be
    Disappointed"
            Signed, Confident!

Found under "The Poet Tree" on a beautiful potted plant ...

"In the midst of flowers
I find myself a part of nature.
I find I'm just a color
I find I'm just a scent &
I find I'm part of God."
Greg

About the Author

When Robert Frost wrote: "Poetry is when an emotion has found its thought and the thought has found words," he might well have been describing the life of desert dweller and sometime Renaissance Man Steve Petersen.

In middle school, a gifted English teacher recognized Steve's ability to paint pictures with words and urged him to try his hand at poetry. The boy's first serious effort, a controversial anti-Vietnam War piece, stirred up both admiration and criticism, as intended.

After graduating from Cal State Northridge on the back of a football scholarship, Steve auditioned for and won membership in the Poetry Society of America. He was subsequently tapped for the innovative Poetry in Motion Program, which involved reading his poems for commuters on Los Angeles' Red Car Transportation System.

In 1992, Steve completed his first novel, *Healer*, the tale of a stranger who miraculously saves the life of a child mangled in an accident, which went on to become an Amazon best seller. Two years later, Steve was named Poet Laureate of the Palm Springs Artist Center, where he came up with one of his most intriguing ideas: the Poet Tree.

"It was conceived as a way of encouraging people, especially children, to embrace language-based artistic experiences," Steve said. "Over the years, it's also turned into a safe place for children to confront difficult emotions and experiences."

In 2001, while flying back to the United States from Mexico mere days after the World Trade Center attacks, Steve penned one of his most memorable pieces, a poem since turned to song called

These Colors Don't Run. Colors, which became an iconic symbol of Operation Iraqi Freedom, is still performed at military events across the country and is currently available on iTunes and Steve's website.

In 2004, Steve was invited to install the first permanent Poet Tree at the Palm Springs Library. Since then, a growing recognition of the importance of art in all its forms to folks of all ages has breathed new life into his creativity. Today, this photogenic and talented man balances work and play, making time for hours-long strolls with his vivacious, wife/manager/agent Vicki as well as working on upcoming Poet Tree projects. His children and grandchildren are top priorities even as he broadens his professional life via readings, singing gigs and a show he wrote, produced and stars in called *The Journey of Life*.

For more information, please visit

**www.stevenpetersen.com or
Steve's author page on Amazon.com.**

Journal Notes

Journal Notes

Journal Notes

Journal Notes

Journal Notes

Journal Notes

Thank you from the center of my  !

If you would like to share and be considered for the next book, please send your creations to:

Steve Petersen Productions, Inc. 501c3
PO Box: 932
Rancho Mirage, Calif. 92270